Images of Westonbirt

Photography by Derek Harris

First Published in 2000
by
The WoodLand & Garden Publishing Company
34 Nene Valley Business Park, Oundle, Peterborough, Cambs, PE8 4HN

Photography Copyright Derek Harris

ISBN 1 899803 14 9

Designed by WoodLand & Garden Publishing Company

Pictures used in this book, other photographic work and prints by Derek Harris are available from
The WoodLand and Garden Picture Library
34 Nene Valley Business Park, Oundle, Peterborough, Cambs, PE8 4HN.
Tel: 01832 270077 Fax: 01832 270088.

Introduction

I don my wellies; and walk through the earthy dew, the scented grass, the music of the birds singing in my ears. Come spring, summer, autumn and winter the tune varies, be it the blackbird, cuckoo, skylark or robin and the scenery too, snowdrops, bluebells, foxgloves and orchids.

Among many varied and special species of flowers the trees stand aloof, so special are they, from evergreens to deciduous, from shrubs to champions.

We have much to enrich our souls, our bodies and minds. Peace of mind is brought to you and the stress of the 21st century is wafted away as you wander through the Arboretum.

I hope memories like these and others are remembered when you turn the pages of this book.

Abigail Carter